D1560264

For Conrad, Kate, and Meg

small poems

by Valerie Worth
pictures by Natalie Babbitt

Farrar, Straus and Giroux   *New York*

Poems copyright © 1972 by Valerie Worth
Pictures copyright © 1972 by Natalie Babbitt
All rights reserved
Library of Congress catalog card number: 72-81488
ISBN 0-374-37072-9
Published simultaneously in Canada by
Doubleday Canada Ltd., Toronto
Printed in the United States of America
Designed by Jane Byers Bierhorst
First edition, 1972

small poems

porches

On the front porch
Chairs sit still;

The table will receive
Summer drinks;

They wait, arranged,
Strange and polite.

On the back porch
Garden tools spill;

An empty basket
Leans to one side;

The watering can
Rusts among friends.

COW

The cow
Coming
Across the grass
Moves
Like a mountain
Toward us;
Her hipbones
Jut
Like sharp
Peaks
Of stone,
Her hoofs
Thump
Like dropped
Rocks:
Almost
Too late
She stops.

zinnias

Zinnias, stout and stiff,
Stand no nonsense: their colors
Stare, their leaves
Grow straight out, their petals
Jut like clipped cardboard,
Round, in neat flat rings.

Even cut and bunched,
Arranged to please us
In the house, in water, they
Will hardly wilt—I know
Someone like zinnias; I wish
I were like zinnias.

chairs

Chairs
Seem
To
Sit
Down
On
Themselves, almost as if
They were people,
Some fat, some thin;
Settled comfortably
On their own seats,
Some even stretch out their arms
To
Rest.

sun

The sun
Is a leaping fire
Too hot
To go near,

But it will still
Lie down
In warm yellow squares
On the floor

Like a flat
Quilt, where
The cat can curl
And purr.

coins

Coins are pleasant
To the hand:

Neat circles, smooth,
A little heavy.

They feel as if
They are worth something.

aquarium

Goldfish
Flash
Gold and silver scales;
They flick and slip away
Under green weed—
But round brown snails
Stick
To the glass
And stay.

pig

The pig is bigger
Than we had thought
And not so pink,
Fringed with white
Hairs that look
Gray, because while
They say a pig is clean,
It is not always; still,
We like this huge, cheerful,
Rich, soft-bellied beast—
It wants to be comfortable,
And does not care much
How the thing is managed.

jewels

In words, in books,
Jewels blaze and stream
Out of heaped chests
Or soft, spilled bags:
Diamonds, sharp stars,
Polished emerald tears,
Amethysts, rubies, opals
Spreading fire-surfaced pools,
Pearls falling down
In foam-ropes, sparks
Of topaz and sapphire strewn
Over a dark cave-floor—
How dim, then, the ring
Worn on the finger,
With one set stone.

tractor

The tractor rests
In the shed,
Dead or asleep,

But with high
Hind wheels
Held so still

We know
It is only waiting,
Ready to leap—

Like a heavy
Brown
Grasshopper.

grass

Grass on the lawn
Says nothing:
Clipped, empty,
Quiet.

Grass in the fields
Whistles, slides,
Casts up a foam
Of seeds,

Tangles itself
With leaves: hides
Whole rustling schools
Of mice.

dog

Under a maple tree
The dog lies down,
Lolls his limp
Tongue, yawns,
Rests his long chin
Carefully between
Front paws;
Looks up, alert;
Chops, with heavy
Jaws, at a slow fly,
Blinks, rolls
On his side,
Sighs, closes
His eyes: sleeps
All afternoon
In his loose skin.

raw carrots

Raw carrots taste
Cool and hard,
Like some crisp metal.

Horses are
Fond of them,
Crunching up

The red gold
With much wet
Juice and noise.

Carrots must taste
To horses
As they do to us.

marbles

Marbles picked up
Heavy by the handful
And held, weighed,
Hard, glossy,
Glassy, cold,
Then poured clicking,
Water-smooth, back
To their bag, seem
Treasure: round jewels,
Slithering gold.

clock

This clock
Has stopped,
Some gear
Or spring
Gone wrong—
Too tight,
Or cracked,
Or choked
With dust;
A year
Has passed
Since last
It said
Ting ting
Or tick
Or tock.
Poor
Clock.

duck

When the neat white
Duck walks like a toy
Out of the water
On yellow rubber-skinned feet,

And speaks wet sounds,
Hardly opening
His round-tipped wooden
Yellow-painted beak,

And wags his tail,
Flicking the last
Glass water-drops
From his flat china back,

Then we would like
To pick him up, take
Him home with us, put him
Away, on a shelf, to keep.

daisies

Where the dusty lane
Wound dull and plain
Among blind weeds,
Today daisies
Have opened a petal-
Decorated way
For us to walk;
The two fluttering, white-
Fringed, golden-eyed banks
Seem wide celebrations—
As if earth were glad
To see us passing here.

pie

After the yellow-white
Pie dough is rolled out
Flat, and picked up
Drooping like a round
Velvet mat, fitted gently
Into the dish, and piled
With sliced, sugared,
Yellow-white apples,
Covered with still another
Soft dough-blanket,
The whole thing trimmed
And tucked in tight, then
It is all so neat, so
Thick and filled and fat,
That we could happily
Eat it up, even
Before it is cooked.

frog

The spotted frog
Sits quite still
On a wet stone;

He is green
With a luster
Of water on his skin;

His back is mossy
With spots, and green
Like moss on a stone;

His gold-circled eyes
Stare hard
Like bright metal rings;

When he leaps
He is like a stone
Thrown into the pond;

Water rings spread
After him, bright circles
Of green, circles of gold.

pebbles

Pebbles belong to no one
Until you pick them up—
Then they are yours.

But which, of all the world's
Mountains of little broken stones,
Will you choose to keep?

The smooth black, the white,
The rough gray with sparks
Shining in its cracks?

Somewhere the best pebble must
Lie hidden, meant for you
If you can find it.

hollyhocks

Hollyhocks stand in clumps
By the doors of old cottages.

Even when one springs alone,
Lost, in an uncut field,

It builds beside it the cottage,
The garden, the old woman, the beehive.

cat

The spotted cat hops
Up to a white radiator-cover
As warm as summer, and there,

Between pots of green leaves growing,
By a window of cold panes showing
Silver of snow thin across the grass,

She settles slight neat muscles
Smoothly down within
Her comfortable fur,

Slips in the ends, front paws,
Tail, until she is readied,
Arranged, shaped for sleep.

fence

The old fence
Has fallen down,
A pile of gray
Rails resting
In the grass.

Where are all
The cows now,
That leaned
Hard there,
Hoping to get out?

Have they pushed
Through, and walked
Down the road,
Past all fences
Forever?

crickets

Crickets
Talk
In the tall
Grass
All
Late summer
Long.
When
Summer
Is gone,
The dry
Grass
Whispers
Alone.